Stevia

55 Naturally Sweetened Recipes

Em Davis

Table of Contents

Introduction

Like many people, I love cakes and cookies and all kinds of sweet breads. But eating these all the time is not healthy, especially if you use sugar, corn syrup, or high fructose corn syrup. Also, if you are diabetic, these foods are on the "do not eat" list.

With the rise of obesity and diabetes in our modern society, I began looking at ways where I could eliminate sugar from my cooking and substitute a more healthy alternative. My quest for healthier living really began after a friend of mine was diagnosed with diabetes. She was later also diagnosed with a gluten sensitivity and a few other health issues that stemmed from her diabetes. I noticed how her life style had to change and how she suddenly couldn't eat certain foods. Not wanting to be there myself, my search for tasty, sugar free food began.

I happened to read about Stevia, a natural plant based, sweetener that is high in fiber and just as sweet as sugar. It does have a bit of an after taste for those who are not used to it. However, I have found that after using stevia for over a year, I no longer notice it and adding a little bit of honey gets rid of any aftertaste.

Stevia is easy enough to find. You can get it at a natural health food store or online.

When I first started using stevia, I noticed that my waistline shrunk some. Also, since stevia is high in fiber, I also noticed that I remained regular in my bowel movements. Anytime I want a sweet treat, I use stevia. I have reached the point where I can no longer stand the taste of sugar, which makes my doctor quite happy. I have eliminated sugary drinks such as soda and fruit juices from my diet. This really pleased my doctor as he referred to soda as "liquid diabetes". Store bought cake and cookies taste like cardboard to me and are too sweet for my taste. Of course, they might taste like cardboard to you too as homemade is always better.

In my efforts to eliminate sugar from my diet, I flipped through my more favorite recipes that I like to make and started changing them a bit to accommodate the usage of stevia. Within this book are those dishes. I included mostly the yeast free breads and desserts and few miscellaneous items such as snacks and beverages.

All of these recipes use stevia extract, but what you choose to use is up to you.

As a side note, I want to mention that I use a gluten free flour blend, but you can use any kind of flour your wish.

My Favorite Breads

Muffins

2 cups gluten free flour

4 tsp. baking powder

¼ tsp. stevia

2 tbsp. honey

¼ cup melted butter

1 cup milk

1. Combine dry ingredients in large mixing bowl. Add liquids and mix until flour is moistened, but do not beat. Batter should be lumpy and a bit thick.

2. Put into muffin pan and bake at 400 degrees for 25 minutes. Makes 12 servings.

Pumpkin Muffins

Use above recipe but substitute 1 cup pumpkin puree for milk.

Pineapple Muffins

1 1/2 cups gluten free flour

3 tbsp. baking powder

1/2 tsp. stevia

1 /12 cups bran (if you don't want to use bran then substitute flour.)

1 egg

1/2 evaporated milk

1/4 cup pineapple juice

1/2 cup crushed pineapple (drained)

1/4 cup melted butter

1. Combine all dry ingredients in bowl. Add remaining ingredients and mix until flour is moistened. Batter should be lumpy.

2. Pour into greased muffin cups and bake at 400 degrees for 25 minutes. Serves 12.

Biscuits

2 cups gluten free flour
¼ tsp stevia
2 tbsp. honey
1-1½ cups milk
1 tbsp. baking powder
½ cup butter

1. Combine dry ingredients. Cut in butter until have tiny flakes. Add liquids and mix well.
2. Drop spoonfuls on a lightly greased baking sheet and bake at 375 degrees for 15-20 minutes.

Cinnamon Rolls

1. Use Biscuit recipe
2. Roll batter on a floured surface until it is ¼ inch thick.
3. Brush with melted butter. Sprinkle cinnamon and stevia on it. Roll into a log.
4. Place on a greased baking sheet and bake at 375 degrees for 15-20 minutes or until golden brown.
5. Drizzle with honey.

Doughnuts

1 tbsp. stevia

4 cups gluten free flour

½ tsp. nutmeg

½ tsp. cinnamon

1 tbsp. melted butter

2 eggs

1 cup milk

4 tsp. baking powder

coconut oil

1. Mix dry ingredients together.

2. In a separate bowl, whisk liquid ingredients together. Add to dry mixture and mix thoroughly.

3. On a floured surface roll dough until it is ½ inch thick. Cut with donut cutter.

4. Heat oil in skillet to 360 degrees. Place donuts in 3 at a time. Turn once when bottom side is golden brown.

5. Place on paper towels to drain when cooked.

6. Serve with honey drizzled on top.

Rice Balls

2 cups cooked rice
3 eggs
1/4 tsp. vanilla
1/2 tsp. stevia
6 tbsp. gluten free flour
3 tsp. baking powder
1/4 tsp. nutmeg

1. Combine rice, eggs, vanilla, and nutmeg.
2. Add flour, stevia, and baking powder
3. Heat oil in a skillet until it is 360 degrees. Add spoonfuls of mixture in it and fry them until they are brown.
4. Remove and place on paper towels to drain.
5. Serve with honey.

Fried Stix

2 tbsp. butter
1 tbsp. stevia
2 eggs
4 cups gluten free flour
1/2 tsp. nutmeg
1 cup cream

1. Cream butter and stevia together. Add eggs, cream, and nutmeg
2. Stir in flour until well mixed
Roll dough on a floured surface until it is 1/2 inch thick. Cut into 1/2 in wide strips.
3. Heat oil in skillet. Fry two strips at a time turning once. When brown on both sides remove from oil and drain on paper towels.
4. Serve plain or with honey.

Griddlecakes

1 1/2 cups gluten free flour

1/2 tsp. baking soda

1 tbsp. stevia

1 egg

5 tbsp. melted butter (or use coconut oil)

1 1/2 cups milk (for a different flavor use buttermilk.)

1. Combine all ingredients and mix thoroughly.

2. On a greased, hot griddle drop spoonfuls of batter. Flip once bottom side is brown.

Serve with favorite syrup.

Waffles

Use Griddlecake recipe and cook in waffle maker according to waffle maker instructions.

Corn Cakes

3/4 cup cornmeal
3/4 cup gluten free flour
2 tsp. stevia
1 tsp. cinnamon
1 tsp. nutmeg
1 egg
1 1/2 cups milk
5 tbsp. melted butter (or coconut oil)

1. Combine all ingredients and blend until smooth. If batter is a bit thick, add milk 2 tbsp. at a time until it is thin enough to pour.
2. Pour spoonfuls of batter on a hot, greased griddle and cook until both sides are brown, flipping once.
3. Serve with favorite syrup

Popovers

1 1/2 cups gluten free flour
2 tbsp. stevia
3 eggs
1 1/2 cups milk

1. Blend flour and stevia together. Add remaining ingredients and mix until smooth.
2. Pour batter in a greased 12 cup muffin pan,.
3. Bake at 450 degrees for 15 minutes. Reduce temperature to 350 degrees and bake 20 minutes more. serve immediately with honey (optional).

Coffee Cake

1 1/2 cups gluten free flour

1 tbsp. stevia

2 tsp. baking powder

3 tbsp. melted butter

1 egg

1/2 tsp. nutmeg

1/4 tsp. cinnamon

2/3 cup milk

1. Combine dry ingredients. Add remaining ingredients and mix just enough to moisten the flour.

2. Pour batter into a greased 9x9 baking pan and bake at 425 degrees for 25 minutes.

Strudel

Filling
8 medium apples (diced)
1/2 cup chopped walnuts (optional)
1 tbsp. stevia
1/4 tsp. nutmeg
1/4 tsp. allspice
2 tsp. cinnamon
2 tbsp. lemon juice
2 tbsp. butter (cut up)
Philo dough (thawed)

1. Combine all ingredients for the filling and mix well.
2. Spread filling on half of the philo dough. Roll into a log.
3. Bake at 375 degrees for 20-30 minutes or until it is golden brown. (Watch it carefully)
4. Cut into slices and serve.

Crepes

Cake

3 eggs

2 tbsp. gluten free flour

1 tbsp. milk

1 tbsp. water

Sauce

3 tbsp. butter

1/2 tbsp. stevia

1/3 cup orange juice

1/2 tsp. grated orange rind (optional)

1. Make the sauce first by mixing all ingredients in a bowl. Set aside.

2. Combines all ingredients for the cake.

3. On a hot greased griddle place spoonfuls of batter and brown on both sides.

4. Add sauce and roll immediately before they cool

French Toast

3 eggs
2 tsp. cinnamon
1/2 tbsp. stevia
1 1/2 cups milk
6 slices of gluten free bread

1. Combine eggs, cinnamon, stevia, and milk and whisk until well blended.
2. Soak bread slices in mixture and place on a hot greased griddle. Brown bother sides.
3. Serve with favorite syrup.

Who Doesn't Like Desert?

Egg Custard

8 eggs

1 cup milk

2 tsp. stevia

1/8 cup honey

1. Whisk all ingredients until well mixed.

2. Pour into an **ungreased** 2 quart casserole dish. Bake at 325 degrees for 40-50 minutes or until a toothpick inserted into the middle comes out clean.

Cheesecake (No Bake)

3 8oz. packages of cream cheese (softened)
1 cup cream
1 tbsp. stevia
1/4 cup honey

1. Mix all ingredients in a bowl with electric mixer until smooth.
2. Pour into a premade pie crust or into a greased spring form cake pan. Put in refrigerator for 12 hours.
3. Serve with fresh fruit on top or plain.

Chocolate Chip Cookies

1 cup butter

1 tbsp. stevia

1/4 cup honey

1/4 cup molasses

1 egg

1 tsp. baking soda

1 tsp. vanilla

1-2 cups gluten free flour

1 12oz package chocolate chips

1. Cream butter, stevia, honey, and molasses in a bowl.
2. Add baking soda, egg, and vanilla.
3. Stir in flour. Dough should be able to hold its shape. If necessary add flour until it does.
4. Mix in chocolate chips.
5. Place 1 tbsp. size balls on a greased cookie sheet. Flatten balls. Bake at 375 degrees for 8-19 minutes or until golden brown.

Oatmeal Cookies

3/4 cups butter
1 1/2 tbsp. stevia
1/4 cup honey
1/4 cup molasses
1 tsp. vanilla
3 cups oatmeal
1 cup gluten free flour (or enough so dough holds its shape)

1. Cream butter, stevia, honey, and molasses. Add vanilla.
2. Stir in oatmeal and flour.
3. Put 1 tsp. size balls of dough on a greased baking sheet. Flatten balls. Bake at 350 degrees for 12-15 minutes or until golden brown. Makes about 2 dozen.

Honey Cookies

2/3 cups butter
1/2 tbsp. stevia
1 cup honey
1 egg
1/2 cup sour cream
1 tsp. baking soda
1 tsp. cinnamon
1 tsp. nutmeg
1 tsp. ginger
1 tsp. allspice
4-5 cups gluten free flour

1. Cream butter, honey, stevia together. Add sour cream, egg, baking soda, and spices.
2. Stir in flour until dough holds its shape.
3. Drop 1 tsp. size balls on a greased baking sheet and flatten. Bake at 37 degrees for 8 minutes or until golden brown. Makes about 2 dozen.

White Cake

2 cups gluten free flour
2 tsp. baking powder
1/2 cup melted butter
1/2 tsp. stevia
1/2 cup honey
1 egg
1/2 cup milk
1 tsp. vanilla

1. Mix dry ingredients together. Add remaining ingredients and mix until smooth.
2. Pour into a greased 9 inch cake pan and bake at 375 degrees for 30-35 minutes or until a toothpick comes out clean.
3. Frost with Cream Cheese Frosting.

Chocolate Cake

1. Add 3/4 cup melted chocolate

Spice Cake

Add 2 tsp. nutmeg, 1 tsp. cinnamon, 4 tsp. ginger, 1/2 tsp. cloves, and 1/2 tsp. allspice.

Applesauce Cake

Use Spice cake variation and substitute applesauce for the butter.

Carrot Cake

Use Spice Cake variation and add 1 cup shredded carrots.

Cream Cheese Frosting

1 8oz package of cream cheese (softened)
1/2 tbsp. stevia
1/8 cup honey
1/4 cup cream

1. Mix all ingredients together with electric mixer until smooth.
2. Frost cake.

Pumpkin Pie

1 pre made pie crust (Or make your own by using 2 cups gluten free flour, or a flour of your choice, 3 tbsp. butter—cut into the flour—and 2 tbsp. cold water.)
1 cup pumpkin puree
1 tsp. ginger
1 tsp. cinnamon
1 tsp. nutmeg
1/2 tbsp. stevia
1/4 cup honey
2-3 tbsp. gluten free flour
1 egg
1 tsp. vanilla

1. Mix all ingredients together in mixing bowl until well blended.
2. Pour into pie crust.
3. Bake at 375 degrees for 40 minutes or until toothpick comes out clean. Wrap edges of pie in foil to prevent it from burning. Serves 8.

Pumpkin Pudding

1. Use recipe above, but use 1 cup flour.
2. Pour into greased 2 quart casserole dish and bake at 375 degrees for 40 minutes or until toothpick comes out clean.

Rice Pudding

1. Use Egg Custard Recipe and pour it over 2 cups of cooked rice that is spread on bottom of baking pan.
2. Bake at 375 degrees for 30-40 minutes or until toothpick comes out clean.

Apple Pudding

4 medium apples (sliced and cored)
1/2 tsp. stevia
1/8 cup honey
1 cup gluten free flour
3/4 cup water
3 tbsp. lemon juice

1. Combine all ingredients in a bowl and mix well.
2. Pour into a 9x9 greased baking pan and bake at 375 degrees for 40-45 minutes or until top has browned.

Spice Pudding

1 cup raisins (optional)
1 egg
1/2 tsp. stevia
2 cups milk
1 tsp. cinnamon
1/2 tsp. allspice
1 tsp. ginger
1/2 tsp. nutmeg
1/2 tsp. cloves
1 tsp. melted butter
3 slices of gluten free bread

1. Toast the bread and crumble into the bottom of a greased baking pan.
2. In a mixing bowl remaining ingredients and mix well. Pour over bread crumbs.
3. Bake at 300 degrees for 30-45 minutes or until a toothpick comes out clean.

Toasted Pecans

1 cup pecans (already shelled)
2 tbsp. melted butter
stevia

1. Spread pecans in a baking pan.
2. Drizzle butter over pecans and sprinkle with stevia.
3. Bake 350 degrees for 15 minutes. Serves about 4.

Vanilla Ice Cream

3 cups cream

1 tsp. stevia

2 tbsp. honey

2 tsp. vanilla

2 egg yokes

1. Combine all ingredients in double boiler and heat until stevia is dissolved. Place in refrigerator for 4 hours.

2. Churn in ice cream maker according to manufacturer's instructions.

Fruit Cobbler

Filling
2 cups of your favorite fruit (sliced)
1/2 tsp. stevia
2 tbsp. honey
1 tbsp. flour
1 tsp. nutmeg (optional)
1 tsp. cinnamon (optional)

Crust
1 cup flout
1/4 cup stevia
1 tbsp. baking powder
1/2 cup butter
1/4 cup milk

For Filling
1. Combine all ingredients and mix until fruit is coated.
Pour into greased 2 quart casserole dish.

For Crust
1. Combine dry ingredients.
2. Cut in butter.
3. Stir in milk. Dough should be somewhat dry, yet hold together.
4. Drop spoonfuls of dough randomly over filling.
5. Bake at 374 degrees for 30-35 minutes or until crust is golden brown.

A Little of This, A Little of That

Kettle Corn

1/2 cup popcorn kernels (popped)
stevia
salt 2-3 tbsp. melted coconut oil

1. Pop popcorn in popcorn maker with 2tsp/ stevia extract and pour into bowl.
2. Drizzle melted oil over popcorn. Sprinkle with salt to taste. Serves 6-8.

Syrup

1/2 cup molasses
1/4 cup honey
1 tbsp. stevia
1 cup pureed fruit (optional)
water if necessary to thin out.

1. Put all ingredients in saucepan and heat until stevia is
dissolved.
2. Remove from heat and serve.

Headache Free Fudge

2 ounces chocolate

1/4 cup butter

3 tbsp. cream

1 egg

1 tsp. vanilla

2 1/2 tbsp. stevia

1/4 cup chopped nuts (optional)

1. Melt chocolate and butter in double boiler stirring constantly
2. Whisk remaining ingredients together. Add to chocolate mixture and beat until smooth.
3. Pour into a buttered pan and chill overnight.
4. Fudge will be gooey and is best serves over ice cream, or some other dessert. Or just scoop out it a spoon and eat straight. Serves 12.

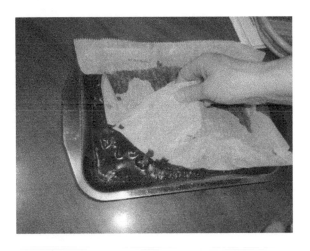

Fruit Pudding

1/2 cup of fruit puree (your favorite fruit)
2 tbsp. stevia
1/4 cup heavy cream

1. Heat fruit puree and stevia in a saucepan until stevia is dissolved. Stir constantly.
2. Whip the cream in a separate bowl and fruit mixture while beating the cream.
3. Carefully put into parfait glasses and chill for two hours before serving.

Baked Citrus

3 large oranges (or any citrus fruit)
3 tbsp. stevia
3 tbsp. butter

1. Wash oranges and grate the skin of each slightly.
2. Cover oranges with water and boil for 30 minutes.
Drain and cool.
3. Removes a small slice from the blossom end and
remove the core.
4. place oranges in a baking pan filled 2/3 way with
water. Put 1 tbsp. stevia and 1 tbsp. butter in each
orange.
5. Cover and bake at 350 degrees for 2 hours. Serves 3.

Orange-Cranberry Relish

1/2 an orange (or apple)
1 cup washed cranberries
1/3 cup stevia
4 tbsp. honey
1/4 cup chopped nuts (optional)

1. Peel orange. Cut into slices and remove membrane and seeds leaving only the pulp.
2. Put the orange pulp, peel, cranberries, stevia, honey, and nuts in food processor until finely chopped.
3. Put into a covered dish and store in refrigerator until ready to serve.

Cranberry Sauce

1 bag of whole cranberries
1 tbsp. stevia
1/4 cup honey
1/4 cup molasses
1/2 cup water

1. Put all ingredients in medium saucepan and stir until well mixed. Heat to boil then turn down heat and let simmer until cranberries have burst and turned into a jelly-like substance. Stir constantly.
2. Serve. Makes 5-6 servings.

Apricot Rice Mold

1 16oz. can apricot halves
1 1/4 tsp. gelatin.
2 cups cooked rice (cold)
2 tbsp. stevia
1/4 cup heavy cream (whipped)
6 custard cups

1. Drain apricots and place a half in bottom of each cup.
Puree remaining halves.
2. Dissolve gelatin according to package instructions and
stir in stevia so it all dissolves together.
3. Combine rice with apricots puree and stir into gelatin.
4. Fold mixture into whipped cream. Pour into custard
cups and chill until firm.
5. Unmold and garnish with whipped cream if desired.

Sweetened Garbanzo Beans

3 cups cooked garbanzo beans
1/4 tsp. stevia
1/3 cup honey
2 tbsp. butter

1. On a large baking pan spread cooked beans until
bottom is covered.
2. Combine honey and stevia and pour over beans. Dot
with butter.
3. Bake at 350 degrees until the liquid is mostly absorbed
and beans are shiny and burnished. (browned)

Glazed Onions

1 pound small white onions
4 tbsp. butter
4 tbsp. honey
2 tbsp. stevia
2 tbsp. fresh chopped parsley

1. Blanch onions in boiling water and drain.
2. Melt butter in a large skillet. Add honey and stevia and stir until mixed.
3. Add onions and cook slowly, turning constantly until they are tender. (about 30-40 minutes)
4. Remove from heat and serve immediately with parsley. Serves about 6.

Glazed Sweet Potatoes

2 pounds sweet potatoes (boiled)
1/2 cup honey
1/2 tbsp. stevia
2 tbsp. molasses
1 1/2 tbsp. butter
1/4 cup pineapple juice

1. Peel and boil sweet potatoes. If they are large, slice them in half lengthwise.
2. Melt butter in skillet. Add remaining ingredients.
3. Add potatoes and cook until they are coated in the glaze. Lower heat if necessary and cook about 15 more minutes, or until moist of the liquid is absorbed.
4. Remove from heat and serve immediately. Serves about 6.

Salad Dressing

6 tbsp. lime juice (lemon juice works too.)
2 tbsp. stevia
2 tbsp. honey
6 tbsp. yogurt

1. Combine all ingredients and mix well. Pour on salad.
Serves 2-3.

Hot Cocoa

2 ounces cocoa powder

2 cups milk

1/4 tsp. stevia

1/3 cup cream

2 tsp. honey

1. Combine all ingredients in saucepan and heat until stevia and cocoa are dissolved, stirring constantly. Do not boil.

2. Pour into cups and serve. Serves 2.

Non-alcoholic Eggnog

6 eggs
4 cups milk
1 tsp. nutmeg
1 1/2 tsp. cinnamon
1 tsp. ginger
1/4 tsp. allspice
3 tbsp. stevia

1. Put all ingredients in blender and blend until smooth.
2. Pour into glasses and add fresh mint leaves. Serves 6.

Fruitade

1/2 tsp. stevia
1 quart water
juice of 1 orange
juice of 1 lime
1/4 tsp. vanilla

1. In a saucepan cook water and stevia until stevia is dissolved. Cool.
2. Add lime and orange juices. Serve over ice.
3. Leftovers can be stored in a sealed container in the refrigerator for 1 day.

Pineapple With a Punch

2 cups milk
2 cups pineapple juice
3/4 cup cream
1/4 tsp. stevia
1 1/2 tsp. lemon juice
1 cup mint tea (freshly brewed and chilled in an ice bath)
2 tbsp. honey

1. Combine all ingredients in bowl and whisk until foamy.
2. Serve immediately. Serves 4-5.

Thank you for purchasing this book.

I hope you find this book a useful resource and enjoy the recipes inside. I make many of them myself and wanted to share them with others, who like me, are trying to go sugar free.

Please consider leaving a review. Reviews help authors and other potential readers.

Once again, thank you.

CPSIA information can be obtained
at www.ICGtesting.com
Printed in the USA
LVHW110213030919
629748LV00001B/134/P